How to Forage & Preserve Food

By: Tristan Trouble

Published in USA by:

CDI Publications, LLC
P.O BOX #9
Boynton Beach
FL 33425

© Copyright 2018

ISBN-13: 978-1717007773
ISBN-10: 1717007775

Table of Contents

Introduction

When it comes to getting food, most of us have the resources we need, at least under normal conditions. Some of us grow our own food, others have a weekly shopping list they carry to the local grocery store once a week, and still others do both, they grow some and shop for the rest. In fact, there are far more people who rely on being able to buy groceries than there are those with the experience to grow their own, and this is a recipe waiting for disaster to strike.

It really doesn't matter what walk of life you come from, or how you go about ensuring the safety and survival of your family, when disaster strikes it places all of us at risk. Granted some of us are more at risk than others, some have better skill sets than others, and some have all the gear and supplies they need to get them through a disaster and keep them alive.

The purpose of this guide is to help level the field so to speak. We are going to cover several food related topics, some of which we will need to do further research on ourselves. This may include purchasing dry goods in bulk, growing vegetables and learning how to can them for future use, just to name a few.

We will discuss how to find wild edibles in all types of environments, from the forest to the centrally located urban park. We will cover what to look for when searching for wild edibles, as well as what to avoid when out hunting for free food. We will also discuss how to properly conduct an edibility test when you come across a plant you are unsure of, and what to do if you consume something toxic. We will also discuss food preservation techniques and how to store surplus in an off grid situation.

This guide will also cover several different types of fishing, some of which are traditional and others that are DIY ideas you can use as a backup during the difficult times of surviving a disaster. Additional coverage will focus on how to hunt small game using conventional and unconventional methods.

This guide will also give a brief overview of starting and maintaining a garden for survival. There are several types of gardens that anyone with a desire can use to start growing food for themselves and their families. The majority of material for this section has been covered in a previously published book, so we will not be giving the gangbuster's version of it here. Suffice to say if you want more information on gardening, we encourage you to grab a copy of our gardening guide.

For those who do not want to grow a garden, or who can't grow a garden due to current living conditions and lack of space, this guide will provide insightful information and recommendations for stockpiling and storing bulk food from emergency preparedness distributors, as well as adopting a rotation schedule to keep your food fresh and useful.

Finally, this guide will cover several conventional and unconventional cooking methods that will come in handy for off grid situations. The information contained in this guide is intended to give the reader the ability to take care of themselves and their families during disaster related events.

Foraging For Wild Edibles

There is no shortage of free food to be found in the forest. In fact, before the industrialization of the food chain in the US, families foraged for food during different seasons to maximize their resources and ensure they had more food than would ever be necessary. Those skills have since perished. Very few US based families actually forage for food on a regular basis anymore. They have grown comfortable and complacent with running to the local grocery store for the things they need.

When people do forage for food in the US, it is more than likely part of a quirky little adventure they participate in with their family. They seldom gather enough food for more than a few meals, if that. In many cases, today's foragers only take what they will be able to use before it spoils or goes bad; they lack the skills to stockpile and store any of that food for future use. While this isn't the best method of foraging for wild edibles, it does give these families the basic skills to find food in the forest should they ever need to, but it does not teach them how many different edibles they are passing by in search of a specific plant.

Some of the wild edibles we will cover in this section are very easy to identify, such as the blackberries featured in the image above; however, many of them are hiding in plain sight and look like nothing more than a plant seeking space on the forest floor. Regardless of what you decide to forage for, and where you decided to forage for it, we highly recommend having a wild edible guide with you when out in the wilderness; this will make it easier to identify potential edibles and avoid plants that are highly toxic to humans when consumed.

Rural Foraging Formalities:

The biggest obstacle to picking a wild plant and eating it is the fact that there are poisonous plants to be aware of, and many of them will grow in close proximity to wild edibles. So, before you grab a handful of that greenery and decide to make a salad for yourself, you need to make sure none of the plants are toxic.

The first recommendation when foraging wild edibles in a rural community is to find a local, or a few locals, who are familiar with the area. People who live in and around small towns often have insightful information about what grows in the woods around them. In many cases, these people conduct seasonal foraging expeditions. They probably start hunting for edible mushrooms in the spring when the weather breaks, and continue walking through the woods looking for acorns, walnuts, hickory nuts, etc. If you can get on their good side, they will show you where to find the wild edibles you've been foraging for, but don't expect them to show or share their favorite spots.

Grab a field guide for the area you will be foraging.

While a mentor is irreplaceable, a guide book will come in very handy should a mentor not be available. A reference resource will help you become more comfortable with looking for wild edibles. It will help you properly identify plants growing in the region, as well as help you prevent picking poisonous varieties from the plant kingdom.

When searching for a guide book on edible plant life, choose one that has the biggest selection of wild edibles for the region you are going to be foraging in. Make sure it has color images that are easy to identify. Black and white photos are extremely difficult to use when trying to identify plants and could lead to misidentification, which could ultimately be fatal. The guide book should also include detailed information on the edibility of the plants in the region, as well as the preferred habitat for finding them.

The first thing you should do with the wild edible reference guide is familiarize yourself with the dangerous plants in the region. If you can properly identify poisonous plant life, then you will feel more confident and comfortable foraging for the edible plants growing in the area.

Learn and use the Latin names of all the plants in your region. Most plants have common names that we are all familiar with; however, several edible plants share the same common name as poisonous plants. Hemlock, for example, can be edible or toxic depending on the variety; "Conium maculatum" refers to the poisonous variety which is highly toxic, whereas "Tsuga canadensis" refers to an edible variety. The Latin language is a dead language, which means it is no longer used for normal day-to-day conversations by anyone on the planet; this makes it an excellent source for naming plants as there is very little opportunity that Latin words and meanings will morph into something new, as is the case with many of the words used in traditional languages today.

When foraging for wild edibles, make sure you are in tune with your surroundings. Don't limit the use of your senses. In many cases, toxic plants have a bitter taste and an acrid aroma; however, this is not the case for all toxic plants. Having said that, an edibility test should only be performed when you are absolutely positive the plant you are about to try is not poisonous. The reason for this is simple, some plants are extremely toxic even in small doses.

Learn what you can about the habitat for the plants you are foraging. This will be hugely beneficial and will help keep you from wasting valuable time in the wilderness looking for something that doesn't grow where you're looking. For example, cattails are edible, and they only grow in certain areas. You will not find cattails growing at high altitudes; they can be found along the edges of ponds and in marshy areas, so looking for them anywhere else will expend energy you cannot replace.

Use your guide book to discover companion plants to

be on the lookout for. This can help you forage for the wild edibles you are after and reduce the time it takes to find and gather them. Take a small notebook with you, or use the reference guide, to make notes about which wild edibles you find growing in close proximity to one another.

Most wild edibles are seasonal, just like the domesticated plants we grow in a garden; there are certain times of the year when they are plentiful and easy to find, and other times of the year when you will have no luck locating them. Know the seasons for foraging wild edibles you are searching for; this will also reduce the amount of time you spend in the woods and should increase your productivity.

Get familiar with all parts of edible plants. Just because one part of a plant is safe for consumption doesn't mean that all parts of the same plant are safe. It may be safe to eat the berries of a certain plant, but not the root, stem, bark, or leaves. In other cases, it is only safe to eat the plant during specific times of the year; once they've gone to seed, they may become toxic.

Forage responsibly and sustainably; never take more plants than you can use, and only take the portions of the plant you need. Wild edibles need to be give the opportunity to replenish naturally since they are not cultivated.

Avoid foraging for wild edibles in areas that may be toxic, such as along roadways, or in areas that have been sprayed heavily with pesticides, chemical based fertilizers, herbicides and/or fungicides. While the plants in these areas may appear healthy, they often absorb the toxic materials through the soil they are planted in.

Never forage wild edibles from nature reserves. These areas have been established to protect wild flora and fauna, so stay out of these areas and allow the plants to repopulate and multiply naturally.

If/when possible, do your part to help wild edible plants repopulate. For example, mushrooms often grow from spores which fall off when the fungus is picked. Use a potato/onion sack with plenty of holes to collect mushrooms, this will allow the spores to fall through the sack and return to the soil, where they have a much better chance of growing again the following season.

When foraging in close proximity to a water source, take time to investigate the water source. If it appears to be polluted, then the plants in the area should also be considered compromised; chances are they will have absorbed toxins from the water source which cannot be removed by washing or cooking. If you are unsure of the water source, avoid consuming wild edibles found in the general vicinity.

Do not forage dead, dying, or diseased plants under

any circumstances. Unhealthy plants can be a sign of hidden toxins. Even if the plants are dying naturally, they should be avoided as they will supply little to no nutritional value.

If the area you plan on foraging isn't state owned land, or land made available for public use, then you should strive to obtain permission before walking the land looking for wild edibles. Most people do not appreciate strangers roaming their grounds regardless of what the reasons are; you could end up in legal trouble or worse.

Always work on improving your foraging skills. Learn new plants and not just the edible varieties; some plants have medicinal purposes that could come in handy as natural remedies you can make from home.

A few general guidelines to follow when you are out learning to forage for wild edibles are;

- ➤ Harvest from plants only after they have sprouted enough foliage to continue growing
- ➤ Harvest plants during the early morning hours once the dew has had time to dry, but long before the heat index for the day reaches maximum
- ➤ Harvest plants before they begin to flower

> Learn to harvest plants at the right time of year, depending on which part and what you plan to use it for

Urban Foraging Formalities:

All of the information provided for rural foraging also applies to urban foraging excursions. However, there are a few things about urban foraging to be aware of that are different from rural foraging expeditions.

Urban foraging has started to gain a little more recognition in recent years. So much so in fact that several major cities in the US now host urban foraging classes designed to provide residents with the ability to identify plants that are considered safe for human consumption, as well as those plants that are considered toxic.

Urban foraging should not be confused with the "freegan" movement, which consists mainly of dumpster diving for edibles that have recently been discarded. The dumpsters of choice are often located behind restaurants in the city and usually include unrefrigerated meat and perishables.

Believe it or not, there are several wild edibles you can find in urban and suburban areas. Mushrooms, nuts, fruit, and even greens grow all over cities in the US, you simply need to know where to go looking for them.

If you live in a suburban area with your own yard, then that's where you should begin foraging for wild edibles. This also applies to condo complexes and apartment buildings as well. All of these areas usually have a "green space," that hosts edible weeds, fruit and nut bearing trees, and shrubbery that might also be beneficial to investigate. Get out into that green space and identify every plant species growing there, then determine if they are edible or poisonous. Remember, if you are unsure, then err on the side of caution and consider the plant poisonous until you can be sure it isn't.

Scout your neighborhood and surrounding environment, basically everything within walking distance of your home. Look for backyards, community gardens, green walls, landscapes, etc., that are full of healthy vegetation. If you locate something that looks promising, then the next step is asking for permission; the last thing you want to do is get picked up for trespassing, and possibly even theft, just because you wanted to pick up a few nuts, berries, or fruits.

Once you have discovered all there is in the immediate vicinity, expand your foraging network to include the rest of the city. Large urban parks, such as Central Park in NYC, may also provide a veritable feast for the urban forager; they're definitely worth taking a look at. Bear in mind that these areas often fall under the supervision of the state parks and recreation department, which means you will need to obtain written permission from said department prior to picking anything from these urban parks.

When foraging an urban area, you also need to be aware of the increased potential for plants to be compromised with environmental toxins. This can occur through the soil or a nearby water source that feeds the area the plants are growing in. Avoid railroads, roadside ditches, medians, golf courses, and sidewalks. These areas can be compromised with anything from industrial waste to dog/cat feces.

Find out what the rules are for foraging the urban area you live in and follow them to the letter; ignorance of the law has never been a suitable defense in a court of law. Some urban areas and parks do not allow foraging at all, during any season or for any reason; others allow restricted foraging by placing limits on the number of wild edibles you can collect per day, week, month, or season.

Do an internet search for foraging groups/clubs/classes in the urban area you reside in; chances are there are already a few set up. Find out when they meet and join them, if for not other reason than to expand your urban foraging knowledge. These groups and the members in them often know the rules for the region, so they will take you to areas where urban foraging is permitted and keep you out of problem areas where foraging may be frowned upon. They will also share an abundance of urban foraging expertise with you along the way, so bring a notebook and pen and be sure to write down everything of importance.

Urban/Suburban Wild Edibles

In wilderness environments there is an abundance of wild edibles to choose from; categorized by region and far too many to list here in this simple guide. However, when it comes to urban wild edibles, the list is rather narrow. There is limited space in urban areas for wild edibles to grow, which means the right conditions have to exist in order for there to even be a chance of finding any. That being said, here are the wild edibles commonly found in urban/suburban environments;

➢ **Clover** - this plant grows everywhere, and identification is rather easy. The blossoms from clover plants can be harvested and eaten fresh or they can be dried and ground into a substitute for flour

> **Acorns** - this nut comes from the oak tree, which can be found throughout urban/suburban landscapes. Acorns are protein rich food sources, but they are also loaded with tannins which must be removed to prevent toxicity to humans.

> **Dandelions** - these plants also grow abundantly throughout urban/suburban areas. Dandelions have been used as ingredients for salads, wines, and even jellies. Pick dandelions before the stalk develops to prevent a bitter taste

➤ **Crabapples** - crab apple trees can be found in certain urban/suburban areas, and although their fruit is not as sweet and flavorful as cultivated apples, they are entirely edible and can usually be foraged straight from the branch

➤ **Roses** - these grow wild as well as cultivated and are considered a wild edible. The petals and the hips of the rose plant are considered edible. They are normally added to baked goods when used as a wild edible food source

> **Mushrooms** - Shaggy Mane, Giant Puffball, Wine Caps, Hen of the Woods, and Oyster Mushrooms (pictured above) are commonly found in urban/suburban settings. Be cautious when foraging for mushrooms as some species are extremely toxic when consumed by humans

> **Daylillies** - these can be found in parks and in neighborhood gardens throughout urban/suburban

areas. You can eat the buds before or after they have opened. They have a sweet, delicate taste

➤ **Raspberries** - this plant grows wherever there is soil to support it. In urban/suburban areas it is not uncommon to find raspberry vines growing near abandoned buildings and lots, or around the edges of neighborhoods, where they butt up to undeveloped land

➢ **Cattails** - these are found around marshy areas and along the edges of small lakes and ponds. It is not uncommon to find them in condo and apartment building complexes that incorporate a pond where wildlife frequently appears

Note: Regardless of where you conduct your foraging experiments, you should also have a foraging app downloaded on your smartphone. Technology has become a beginning forager's best friend, so use it to your advantage when on the trail. These apps serve as quick reference guides that are easier to carry than the wild edible picture book you have been using to familiarize yourself with the plants growing in your area!

The Universal Edibility Test:

Before we discuss how to properly conduct an edibility test, we should mention that this type of test should ONLY be conducted as a last resort, in a serious life/death situation, on plants you are not familiar with. Be aware that plants consist of various parts; some of which are edible, others which may be toxic, and these can be from the same plant. Do not make the mistake of assuming an entire plant is edible simply because one part of it passed the edibility test.

The parts of a plant are as follows:

> ➤ Fruit/Seeds (this includes berries and nuts)
> ➤ Stems/Stalks
> ➤ Leaves
> ➤ Flowers
> ➤ Roots

Before conducting an edibility test on a new plant, you must first separate it into the various parts listed above. Once you have separated the plant accordingly, you are ready to conduct the edibility test. Because different parts of the same plant can be edible or toxic, you must conduct an edibility test on each part of the plant, but never simultaneously. Each part of the plant is tested individually until it has been determined edible or toxic.

Here are some early identifiers that may alert you to the possible toxicity of an unfamiliar plant. The following plants should never be subjected to an edibility test, under any circumstances:

- Mushrooms that you are not intimately familiar with. Certain mushroom species are extremely toxic, especially to humans, so if you aren't 100% sure about what you're looking at, avoid it altogether. Don't even touch it!
- Plants that are in close proximity to a polluted body of water. Even if the plants appear healthy, there is a good chance they have absorbed harmful toxins from the water supply through their root system
- Plants that bear slick and shiny leaves are often poisonous
- Plants that bear 3-leaf patterns should be avoided as they can be toxic as well
- Plants that sting when they are touched are normally not edible for humans
- Plants that exhibit a strong, foul aroma should be considered toxic and avoided
- Plants that initially taste soapy or bitter should be avoided

- ➤ Plants that bleed milky white sap from the stems when picked, are often toxic
- ➤ Any seeds from pods should be avoided
- ➤ All grains that come from plants with pink, purple, or black spurs

Listed below are some pre-edibility steps to take. When conducted properly, an edibility test will take several days. These will ensure a successful edibility test while also reducing the possibility of unnecessary exposure and maximizing the results of the test itself:

- ➤ Choose a plant that is growing in abundance. Conducting an edibility test on plants that are hard to find, places you at risk unnecessarily. By conducting the edibility test on plants that are plentiful, you increase your potential food supply
- ➤ Fast for 8 hours before conducting the initial edibility test
- ➤ Drink nothing but water for the entire duration of the edibility test, and do not eat anything besides the part of the plant being tested. This will help ensure that the results of the test are from the plant itself and not something else you ingested

The universal edibility test itself has several steps that must be taken as described. Do not attempt to cut corners as doing so could place you, and anyone else relying on you, at great risk. Remember, each part of the plant needs to be tested individually and separately.

> ➤ Cook the plant part you want to test first. While raw consumption may be possible, cooking the plant part often removes, or reduces, chemical compounds and harmful pathogens that may be present and hazardous to consume
> ➤ Allow the plant part to cool, then touch it to an exposed area of skin; do you experience a burning sensation? If yes, discontinue the test and discard that part of the plant, consider it toxic. If no, continue on with next step
> ➤ Wait 3-5 minutes and inspect the area of skin for signs of redness or rash. If there are signs of a rash, discontinue the test and discard that plant part, consider it toxic. If no signs appear, continue on with next step
> ➤ Place the cooked yet cooled plant part on a new area of skin and allow to remain in contact for a period of 15 minutes. Remove plant part and recheck for signs of burning, itching, redness, swelling, or rash. If signs are present, discontinue test and discard plant part, consider it toxic. If no signs appear, continue with next step
> ➤ Touch plant part to the exterior portion of your lip, upper or lower, but not necessarily both. Monitor the area where the plant was placed for a period of 15 minutes and check for any reaction. If an adverse reaction occurs, discontinue test and discard plant part, consider it toxic. If no adverse reaction is present, then continue on with next step
> ➤ Place a small portion of the plant part on your tongue and allow it to sit there for 15 minutes, but

do not chew the plant part. Spit it out and inspect the area of your tongue for any adverse reaction. If signs are present, discontinue testing and discard plant part, consider it toxic. If no signs of reaction continue with next step

➤ Chew a small portion of the plant part for at least 15 minutes, but do not swallow

➤ If there are no signs of adverse reaction after 15 minutes, then swallow that small portion

➤ Wait for at least 8 hours to determine any adverse reactions. If you experience any abdominal pain or vomiting, then drink plenty of water and discontinue eating that part of the plant.

➤ If no signs are present at the end of 8 hours, then consume approximately ¼ cup of the plant parts and wait an additional 8 hours

➤ If there are no negative reactions after this 8 hour period, then that part of the plant can be considered safe for human consumption

➤ Consume the plant part in small quantities, even if you have proven it safe for human consumption, as your body will need time to adjust to this new addition to the diet

Food Preservation Techniques

Once you've learned to master the method of gathering wild edibles, you may need to preserve and store the food for future use. The techniques presented here can be used for wild edibles, or for conventional bulk purchases of raw food.

If you practice sustainable foraging throughout the year, gathering only enough for immediate personal use, then you may not need to preserve or store your wild edibles. However, if you are ever forced to forage for daily sustenance, these food preservation techniques will come in handy.

You can also use these food preservation techniques to save money on your annual grocery bill by purchasing raw food in bulk. You can find most, if not all, of the produce you will ever need for an entire year at a local Farmer's Market. Likewise, you can buy meat products in bulk as well and preserve it to last you throughout the year. If you do not have a local butcher you are familiar with, check local listings for a meat market, or ask a local homesteader where they take their livestock to be processed.

Food preservation methods represent a very valuable set of prepper skills. Many of us no longer use these skills because we shop from a local grocery store and the processing has been taken care of for us; this will place the majority of us at risk. Food borne allergies and illnesses arise from processing problems along the industrial food chain. We remove these threats when we take matters into our own hands and grow/forage for the food we need, then process and store it for future use. When done properly, these techniques ensure a safe food source by eliminating added preservatives and lax handling regulations.

The skills required to preserve and store your own food may also come in handy if you are a prepper. One of the tenets of emergency preparedness is to ensure that you have enough food, water, and additional supplies to withstand a lengthy grid down situation. While you might be able to get by with nothing more than bulk purchases at first, should the grid down situation last longer than your supplies, you will need a way to supplement them. If you do not have food preservation skills if/when that occurs, then you will have to hunt, fish, and forage on a daily basis just to survive, which will leave you very little time to do anything else.

Most of us are familiar with temporary food preservation techniques; we've all dumped an open box of food into a Tupperware container and closed the lid to keep it fresh long enough to put it into use. To perform the food preservation and storage techniques presented in this portion of the guide, you will need special equipment. The techniques for canning and dehydrating can be used during normal times as well as during grid down situations.

The techniques for freeze drying food require the use of a freezer or dry ice, so you may not be able to use this method effectively in a lengthy grid down situation; however, should you decided to freeze dry food now and add it to your surplus, it can be kept just below room temperature once the freeze drying process has been completed.

How to Can Food

When it comes to using the canning method to preserve food, there are two methods you can use. One is referred to as "Water Bath Canning," and the other is called "Pressure Canning." We will discuss how to use both methods so that readers have the ability to choose what works best for them, depending on their needs and available equipment.

The Water Bath Canning Method:

Basically, the hot water bath canning method consists of using a large pot that has a small rack sitting on the bottom. Food is placed in canning jars, which are then secured with special canning lids, then the jars are submersed in boiling hot water for the specified time period. Once the jars have been processed according to the water bath canning recipe used, the jars are removed from the water bath and allowed to cool, at which time the vacuum seal is created. Bear in mind that this method of canning food only heats the food to a temperature equivalent to that of boiling water.

Step 1

The first order of business is making sure you are using the right canning method for the food you want to preserve. Not all foods can be properly canned and preserved using this method. Water bath canning is a relatively simple and easy method. It should be used to can foods/fruits that are highly acidic, such as pickles, fruit bathed in syrup, jams, jellies, and preserves.

Meat/poultry/fish/vegetables/soup stock should all be processed using the pressure canning method discussed later in this guide. Regardless of what is being canned using this method, always make sure that recipe you are using is from a trusted and reliable source, such as the *National Center for Home Food Preservation*.

Step 2

You will need some basic canning equipment. Most hardware stores, big box as well as local, carry ready-to-use canning kits, which can also be purchased online. However, you may want to take inventory of the equipment you already have in the kitchen and purchase any additional items individually in order to save money. Here is a list of the equipment you will need for water bath canning:

- A large stock pot (a tall one if possible)
- A small rack that fits into the bottom of the large stock pot
- Canning jars with canning lids (often sold together or in close proximity)
- A food grade funnel
- A ladle
- A kitchen timer
- A canning jar lifter (tongs may be used as a substitute, but they are riskier)

> ➢ Paper towels, moistened
> ➢ A clean spatula

Step 3

Separate the jars from the lids and rings. Set the jars on the rack inside the stock pot. Add enough water to the pot to cover the jars by approximately one inch. Bring the water to a simmer and keep the jars at this temperature. Preheating the jars this way will help keep them from breaking when hot food is added.

Step 4

Get your recipe out and prepare the food. When you have the recipe ready, use a jar lifter or tongs to remove the jars. Pour the warm water from the jars back into the simmering pot. Set the jars on a cloth on top of the kitchen counter or workspace. Use the food grade funnel to fill the jars, but make sure to leave enough headspace recommended by the recipe; normally ¼ to ½ inch (this is an air gap between the top of the food and the lip of the jar).

Step 5

Once the food has been added to the jars and they've been filled, wipe off the rim of each jar to ensure it is clean and dry. Now, take a lid for each of the full jars and center it on top, then take a ring and secure the lid until finger tight.

Step 6

Next, place the lidded jars back into the stock pot and arrange them on the rack. Make sure the water in the pot covers the jars and return to a boil. Set the timer according to the instructions of the recipe and allow them to be processed. When the time sounds, carefully remove the jars using a jar lifter or tongs and place them upright on a clean dry towel. If you listen carefully you should hear the lids "pop" into place as the vacuum seal is created.

Step 7

Allow the jars to cool for a period of 12-24 hours depending on recipe instructions, then remove the rings and check to ensure the lids are secured in place. Label those jars with a good seal and store them in the pantry/basement/root cellar until they are ready to be used.

Note: If any of the jars has a lid that isn't sealed properly, place it in the refrigerator and use it as soon as possible to prevent spoilage and waste.

The Pressure Canning Method:

This method of canning consists of filling jars with raw food that has not been preheated. The food is placed inside jars along with boiling hot water/syrup/juice, then the jars are sealed and placed inside a pressure canner for a specified period of time to finish the processing. Once the jars of food have been processed they are removed from the pressure canner and allowed to cool before they are added to the pantry stock. This method is usually used with meat, poultry, fish, vegetables, etc. While water bath canning heats the food to 212°F (the temp of boiling water), the pressure canning method heats the food to 240°F.

Step 1

Refer to Step 1 of Water Bath Canning above; the same applies to Pressure Canning.

Step 2

You will need pressure canning equipment. Refer to Step 2 of Water Bath Canning above; you will need all that equipment, but you will need a pressure canner instead of a large stock pot. A pressure canner is not the same as a pressure cooker.

Step 3

Find a recipe from a reliable source and gather all the equipment and ingredients you are going to need; arrange them accordingly in the kitchen/workspace.

Step 4

Inspect the jars, rings, and lids to ensure they are free from cracks, nicks, and/or sharp edges along the rim that weren't ground down properly. Remove any jar, ring, lid that shows signs of damage and discard (this defective equipment could cause further damage, and possibly even personal injury, if used in a pressure canner). Wash jars, rings, lids in hot soapy water; then rinse and dry lids and rings.

Step 5

Place jars in a large stock pot and fill with water. Bring the water to a simmer and leave jars in the warm water until you are ready to use them. Leave the rings and lids at room temperature during this step. Preheating the jars keeps them from breaking when the hot food is introduced later.

Step 6

Place the pressure canner on the stove over medium-high heat and add 2-3 inches of water. Bring water to a simmer and keep it there until the canning jars have been filled with food and are ready to be placed in the pressure canner.

Step 7

Prepare the recipe as instructed; do not cut corners, especially if you are new to canning. Use a jar lifter or tongs to remove a single jar from the hot water. Use the food grade funnel to fill the jar with prepared food, allowing adequate headspace as described in the recipe being followed. Use the spatula to remove air bubbles if instructed by the recipe. Continue releasing trapped air 2-3 times around the jar.

Step 8

Wipe down the edge and threads of each jar as soon as you have them filled with food and the air has been released. Center lids onto the jars and secure with rings until finger tight. Arrange jars inside pressure canner until the canner is full, or the recipe and ingredients have all been exhausted. Make sure the water level is 2-3 inches high, or as instructed in the recipe.

Step 9

Place the lid on the pressure canner and secure it in place; make sure to leave the vent open. Turn heat up to medium-high and let the steam escape through the vent. When the escaping steam creates a steady stream, set timer for 10 minutes and allow to vent; ensuring that there is no air left in canner, only steam. Close the vent and adjust heat gradually until recommended pressure is achieved and maintained.

Step 10

Leave jars at recommended pressure for suggested time period found in the recipe being followed. Remove canner from heat and allow to stand until pressure returns to zero on its own. Once pressure has returned to zero, wait 10 minutes then remove the locking mechanism and open lid; be careful to tilt it away from you to prevent personal injury. Once the lid of the pressure canner has been removed, wait another 10 minutes for jars to start cooling.

Step 11

Using a jar lifter or tongs, remove the jars from the pressure canner and place on a clean towel on the kitchen counter or workspace. Allow the jars to sit for 12-24 hours; do not disturb them!

Step 12

Inspect the lids to ensure they have properly sealed.

The lids should remain stable when pressing the center; if they flex up and down the seal has failed, remove this jar from the rest and place in the refrigerator. Use this jar of food as soon as possible to prevent spoilage and waste. Remove the rings from the jars with sealed lids, label them and place them in the pantry/basement/root cellar until ready to use.

Hot Packing vs. Cold Packing:

In addition to water bath canning and pressure canning, you should also be aware of the difference between "hot packing," and "cold packing." This may or may not be included in the recipe instructions; here's a brief description of both;

> ➤ **Hot Packing** - this method consists of canning food that has been freshly boiled. The boiled food is placed inside the jar after which boiled water/syrup/juice is also added to the jar and it is processed according to the recipe being followed. The hot packing method is most often used with water bath canning recipes. This process helps reduce the amount of air present in raw food, which

also helps improve overall shelf life of the finished product

➤ **Cold Packing -** this method consists of canning raw food that has been prepared, but not preheated. This process is also referred to as "raw packing," as raw food is placed in hot jars, after which boiling water/syrup/juice is added to the jars allowing for adequate headspace. These jars are then further processed using a pressure canner. This method does not remove the amount of air normally found in raw food so there may be some discoloration to the packaged product after it has sat on a shelf in the pantry for 2-3 months

How to Dehydrate Food

Drying food is one of the oldest food preservation techniques known to man. Man has learned to use the sun, a smoky fire, and even the wind to dry all manner of food for preservation, including fruits, berries, grains, meats, poultries, fish, and herbs.

Basically, food dehydration consists of removing all water content from food through hot air circulation which prevents the opportunity for bacterial growth. Dehydrated food is lightweight due to water removal. It is very simple to prepare, store, and use; as an added bonus it is also very nutritious and flavorful. Dehydrated foods are fiber rich and a great source of carbohydrates, yet extremely low fat, which makes them a very healthy choice.

Dehydrating food requires less energy and preparation than freeze drying or canning, and the finished product requires far less storage space. Once food has been dehydrated it should be stored in a cool, dry place until ready for use.

There are several methods for drying food, many of which we will cover here. Some of these methods are conventional; they require electricity or special equipment such as an oven or dehydrator, whereas other methods will be unconventional and may require the construction of special equipment in order to compensate for a lack of electricity.

Sun & Air Drying

This is perhaps the oldest known method of drying food. Long before man discovered fire and made good use of it, he had to hang food in a warm air current in order to remove the water from it and keep it suitable for human consumption.

This method can still be used today. If you live in a region where the days are long, hot, and full of sun, then this process will be rather easy to complete. Find a recipe from a respected resource and adhere to all instructions. This method is risky if not performed correctly and is generally only recommended for fruit.

To dry fruit in the sun, an outdoor temperature of at least 86°F is required, and a slight breeze wouldn't hurt matters at all. It also wouldn't hurt if the relative humidity remained below 60%. The fruit to be dried needs to be placed on a rack, or a screened tray, to provide adequate air flow. Outdoor dehydration racks can be made out of wood; however, green wood, redwoods, cedars, pines, and oaks should be avoided as they can leech into the food.

The variables for sun and air drying are too vast to try and provide accurate coverage for all readers ad the regions they live in. Prior to attempting this food drying process it is highly recommended that you find a recipe from a respected resource and/or an instructional video on the food you want to dry using this method.

Fire Drying

This is perhaps the second oldest method of preserving food known to man. Once man was able to harness the power of fire he quickly began using it for things like drying food. Again, this method is rather risky, but can still be performed today.

In order to use this process for preserving food it will be necessary to build a fire out of hardwood; softwood will taint the food. Again, you will want to find a recipe specifically for drying the food you have in mind, using this method. This method is often used for drying meats.

The basic process involves building a fire and allowing

it to burn down to hot coals. The meat to be dried is cut into thin strips, no thicker than ¼ inch with all the fat removed. The meat strips are then marinated in a salt/water mixture; $1/8^{th}$ cup salt to 1 quart of water. This marinating process lasts for one hour and the meat strips need to be stirred every 15 minutes to ensure salt water saturation.

Once the fire has reduced to hot coals, the meat strips are hung 2-3 feet above the coals on a pole or wire. You should be able to place your hand near the meat and feel the heat, but not experience burning; remember that you're trying to dry the meat, not cook it and this requires just enough warm air circulating to prevent microorganisms from making the meat useless.

Adding damp hardwood chips will create a smoke that will protect the meat from insects and birds. The coals will need to continue burning for several hours in order for the drying process to complete, so you will have to add fuel to the fire base occasionally or keep a separate fire pit going to take coals from when needed.

Solar Dehydrators

Solar dehydrators normally consist of homemade designs that incorporate a shelving rack system with a piece of Plexiglas. There are several design options available through online resources. These devices are similar to sun and air drying as they do use both; the biggest difference is the enclosed environment inherent to the solar dehydrator design, which offers a greater level of protection for the food being dried.

Solar dehydrators use material to increase interior temperatures and improve ventilation, which results in much quicker drying times. Quicker drying times help prevent mold and bacterial growth as well as reduce the amount of spoilage.

Conventional Dehydrator

As this is a conventional technique that doesn't require the use of sun or outdoor environments, we will discuss this in greater detail as many of the instructions will be similar. Using a conventional dehydrator is one of the simplest ways to dehydrate food, especially if you've never done it before. This is also a great way to ensure you have enough food stockpiled for the year. As always, find a recipe from a respected resource for the food you want to dry. Before you can use this method, you will need a few pieces of equipment:

> ➢ A high quality dehydrator (don't buy the cheapest thing you can find, buy once and buy right, more on that later)
> ➢ A sharp knife for cutting fruit, vegetables, and meat
> ➢ A cutting board
> ➢ Air tight freezer bags or other containers
> ➢ Sugar/Salt (optional)
> ➢ Citric Acid/Ascorbic Acid (optional)
> ➢ Small pot to blanch vegetables in

A high quality dehydrator will have excellent air flow, a dual heating element, and a good fan. Air flow and temperature control are the most significant components of a good food dehydrator. Multiple tray capacity is also a plus, as is having an adjustable thermostat and even heat distribution. Look for trays that will make cleaning easy to accomplish and you'll be all set.

Step 1

Use the freshest food possible and only that of high quality. Any food that is overripe, or near expiration should be avoided, as should bruised or damaged food; all of these conditions lead to dissatisfying results.

Step 2

Clean, hull, slice, or trim the vegetables, fruits and meats; try to maintain thickness consistency as this will ensure the food dehydrates evenly.

Step 3

If dehydrating fruits that are vulnerable to oxidation, consider using citric/ascorbic acid; this will help retain color of the fruit throughout the entire process.

Step 4

If dehydrating vegetables, blanche them first; this helps retain color and quickens the drying time. Place vegetables in boiling water for 3-5 minutes to blanche sufficiently for this process

Step 5

Line food slices onto trays making sure not to overlap and add salt/sugar if desired. Turn on the dehydrator according to owner's manual and adhere to drying times recommended by manual and/or recipe. Normal drying times range between 8-12 hours.

Step 6

After the recommended drying time, inspect several pieces of food to determine dryness. Cut a handful of slices in half and look for signs of moisture. If there are no signs of moisture, then the food is adequately dried. If there are signs of moisture, then return them to the dehydrator and check them hourly until they are sufficiently dried.

Step 7

Remove trays from dehydrator and allow food to cool for 30-60 minutes; the food slices should be room temperature before being stored.

Step 8

Place the dried food into air tight freezer bags or other containers. This food needs to be stored in a cool dry place until you want to consume it.

Using an Oven

This is another conventional method that can be used to dehydrate all types of food. This process may be used as a substitute for using a conventional dehydrator as described and detailed above. This drying process will require frequent supervision and monitoring to prevent the food from getting to dry. If you are going to use this method, find recipes from reliable resources for the foods you want to dehydrate using the type of oven you have available (gas/electric). Prior to using this method, you will need a few items:

> ➢ A small fan to help with air flow and circulation
> ➢ Sharp knives for slicing food
> ➢ Lemon juice for fruits
> ➢ A small pot for blanching vegetables
> ➢ Cooking pans/sheets
> ➢ An oven

When using an oven, you want to use the lowest temperature possible, yet still get the job done. You also want to make sure the temperature isn't so high that it cooks the food rather than dries it. The recommended temperature ranges between 140-200°F.

Step 1

Prepare your food by washing it, peeling it, hulling it, trimming the fat off, slicing it, etc. Remove all damaged areas of food and any seeds/cores.

Step 2

If dehydrating vegetables, blanch them first. This helps retain color, flavor, and texture. Boil in water for 3-5 minutes then submerse them in ice cold water until the vegetables are cool to the touch. Remove the vegetables, pat them dry, and arrange them in a single layer on a cooking pan/sheet.

Step 3

If dehydrating fruits, soak them in water and lemon juice for 60 seconds to help retain color and flavor, then remove them and pat dry before arranging in a single layer on a cooking pan/sheet.

Step 4

Place the cooking sheet in the oven and adjust temperature to 140°F. If your oven doesn't have a setting this low, then use the "Warm" setting and keep an eye on the drying process.

Step 5

Leave the door of the oven cracked open several inches. Place the fan so it is blowing air into the opening of the oven door; this helps with air flow and circulation.

Step 6

Refer to the recipe being followed for drying times.

When the drying time has been reached, remove the cooking pan/sheet from the oven and inspect the food for dryness. Cut into several slices and inspect for moisture. If moisture is present, continue dehydrating in the oven. If no moisture is present, then remove and allow food to cool for 30-60 minutes.

Step 7

When food has cooled, remove and place in an air tight container or freezer bag and store in a cool dry place until ready to consume.

Food Foraging, Preservation, & Storage Tips

The purpose of foraging for food is to substitute/supplement the food you are able to grow or purchase yourself. When foraging always adhere to sustainable practices for the plants you are picking; you want them to grow again in the same area the following year so that they are easier to find when the season arrives.

Foraging is an exercise and an adventure all-in-one. Chances are you will be bringing items with you that will need to be discarded, such as water bottles and food wrappers; there is a place for this rubbish and it isn't in the wilderness. Always take with you what you brought with you and leave nothing behind except the seeds/spores of the plants you've picked. Never harvest more than you can preserve or use within a year.

When preserving food, always adhere to safe practices. Use clean work environments and protective gear, such as gloves, to prevent the spread of germs and bacteria. If you're going to put forth this much effort to ensure you have enough food for an entire year, then you'll want to make sure the effort is not wasted through spoilage.

Food preservation allows you to save an enormous amount of money on the yearly food bill, regardless of how you obtain the food, through foraging or bulk purchases from Farmer's Markets. Food preservation also allows you to control what food you eat, as well as what goes into the food you eat; you can get rid of GMO's, pesticides, herbicides, fungicides, etc., and eat healthy wholesome food every day.

All canned and dehydrated food should be stored in a cool dry place until ready to use. Keep it out of the sunlight as this will cause the food to begin breaking down quicker than it should. If you have a pantry, then develop a rotation schedule for the food you have stored there. If you have a root cellar, make sure you are rotating your stock in there as well.

Several of the topics covered in this guide contain variables that are too numerous to cover for each region. The wild edibles you find in Oregon are going to be far different than those found in Florida. Much of this information is intended to point you in the right direction for further research and discovery.

If/when possible, find a local mentor to assist you with your foraging and food preservation techniques; these folks have invaluable knowledge with regards to regional foraging delicacies and the various food preservation techniques that work the best.

Food Storage

Food storage is an extremely important aspect of developing an annual surplus food plan. Without proper storage your surplus food will be at greater risk of spoiling, being infested with insects, subject to bacterial growth, and/or eaten by varmints.

Before you begin the process of obtaining surplus food you should make sure you have the space to stockpile in safely and securely. If you don't have the space, you will need to make space, or build it.

There are basically three methods for storing surplus food that should be given serious consideration; the food pantry, a spare room in the basement, and/or an outdoor root cellar. Regardless of what you use, the surplus food must be stored in airtight containers that are animal and insect proof. Even if you purchase dry goods in bulk, they normally need to be taken out of their packages and placed into new airtight containers if they are going to be stored for any length of time.

If all you have is a food pantry at your disposal, then your food storage plan might need to incorporate refilling and rotating stock a couple times a year. A food pantry can be any room that maintains a cool, dry, and dark environment, such as a walk-in closet. This room shouldn't have access to sunlight, or the outdoors, and should have ample shelving to make things run smoothly. Any spare closet will suffice but the closer it is to the kitchen the easier it will be to use.

Any spare room in the basement that doesn't have appliances, such as a hot water heater, air flow exchanger, etc., and that mimics a large closet without windows and access to the outdoors, can be used for long term food storage. This type of room can serve as the general pantry from which food is rotated into the kitchen pantry or cupboards when needed.

A root cellar is the oldest method of storing food known to man. Root cellars are underground rooms you must dig and build yourself. They are designed specifically for the long-term storage of food. There are several root cellar plans and configurations to consider, some of which serve a multipurpose function by doubling as storm shelters. Root cellars are built outdoors which means that ALL food stored inside them must be in animal/insect proof airtight containers; anything short of that will not last long enough to be consumed and will more than likely attract unwanted attention from hungry wildlife in the area.

Remember, that no matter which food storage option you decide to go with, you should never stockpile more food than you can use in a single year. Even if you purchase bulk food from an emergency preparedness provider with a shelf life of 25 years, it is a good idea to put it into rotation and use it as you would any other food source. While an extended shelf life is a great piece of advertising eye candy, very few people will want to open a 25 year old package of food, and that includes the person buying and storing it for that long; not to mention the fact that within that 25 year window there will more than likely be upgrades and improvements to bulk surplus foods designed for the emergency preparedness community.

ALL RIGHTS RESERVED. No part of this publication may be reproduced or transmitted in any form whatsoever, electronic, or mechanical, including photocopying, recording, or by any informational storage or retrieval system without express written, dated and signed permission from the author.

DISCLAIMER AND/OR LEGAL NOTICES: Every effort has been made to accurately represent this book and it's potential. Results vary with every individual, and your results may or may not be different from those depicted. No promises, guarantees or warranties, whether stated or implied, have been made that you will produce any specific result from this book. Your efforts are individual and unique, and may vary from those shown. Your success depends on your efforts, background and motivation. The material in this publication is provided for educational and informational purposes only. Use of the programs, advice, and information contained in this book is at the sole discretion and risk of the reader.